AF802743

LAWS

—— Of The ——

Choctaw Nation

—— Passed At The ——

Regular Session of the General Council

—— CONVENED AT ——

Tushka Humma

October 3rd, 1892, and Adjourned November 4th, 1892.

—— o ——

LAWS

—OF THE—

Choctaw Nation

—PASSED AT THE—

Regular Session of the General Council

—CONVENED AT—

TUSHKA HOMMA,

Oct. 2, 1893, and Adjourned Oct. 27, 1893,

—AND THE—

SPECIAL SESSIONS

CONVENED IN FEBRUARY 1892

—AND—

CONVENED IN JUNE, 1893.

SR Scholarly Resources Inc.
1508 Pennsylvania Avenue Wilmington, Delaware 19806

WITHDRAWN
FROM
NEW MEXICO STATE UNIVERSITY
LIBRARY

SCHOLARLY RESOURCES, INC.
Wilmington, Delaware • London

Reprint edition published in 1975

Library of Congress Catalog Card Number: 75-3689
ISBN: 0-8420-1880-8

Manufactured in the United States of America

E
99
.C8
.C579
1975
c. 2

LAWS

—Of The—

Choctaw Nation

—Passed At The—

Regular Session of the General Council

—CONVENED AT—

Tushka Humma

October 3rd, 1892, and Adjourned November 4th, 1892.

—o—

ATOKA, IND. TER.
INDIAN CITIZEN PUBLISHING CO.
1893

397057

NEW MEXICO STATE UNIVERSITY LIBRARY

LAWS OF THE

CHOCTAW NATION, REGULAR SESSION.

1892.

BILL NO. 1.

Be it resolved by the Senate and House of Representatives in General Council assembled, That no one but members of Council, and the officers connected therewith, shall be present during the counting of the votes for Principal Chief.

Be, it further resolved, That the Principal Chief request the U. S. Indian Agent to have the U. S. Soldiers to co-operate with the National Lighthorsemen in guarding both entrances of the yard around the capitol and prohibit all persons, except those designated above, from entering the building during the counting of the votes.

And that this resolution take effect and be in force from and after its passage.

Apppoved October 5th 1892.

W. N. JONES,
P. C. C. N.

BILL NO. 2.

SECTION 1. Be it enacted by the General Council of the Choctaw Nation assembled, That the sum of ($50) fifty dollars, is hereby appropriated out of any money in the National Treasury, not otherwise appropriated, to pay Ellis Bohanan for taking care of Tushka Homma Female Institute for (50) fifty days previous to its occupancy by the Superintendent.

SEC. 2. And that this Act take effect and be in force from and after its passage.

Approved.

W. N. JONES,
P. C. C. N.

BILL NO. 3.

An Act to increase the pay of National Lighthorsemen.

Be it enacted by the General Council of the Choctaw Nation assembled, That section XI of Chapter II fixing the salary of National Lighthorsemen, be so amended as to increase unto three dollars and fifty cents for each and every days actual attendance on the General Council.

This Act shall take effect and be in force from and after its passage.

Approved Oct. 12th 1892.

W. N. JONES,
P. C. C. N.

BILL NO. 4.

A resolution of respect tendered to the late B F. Smallwood Ex-Principal Chief of the Choctaw Nation.

Whereas, the unwelcome Messenger death has again visited our midst and laid his icy claws upon the honored body of our esteemed friend and former Chief the Hon. B. F. Smallwood, who departed this life on the 15th day of December 1891; And while we bow with humble submission to the wise dispensation of Him who doeth all things well, yet with sad heart we mourn the loss of one who so long served his people faithfully and vacated the office of Principal Chief of the Choctaw Nation with honor, and always had the interest of his people at heart: Therefore.

SECTION 1. Be it resolved by the General Council of the Choctaw Nation assembled, That both Houses of the General Council adjourn until Tuesday morning at 9 o'clock A. M. the 18th day of Oct., 1892, out of respect to the deceased B.

F. Smallwood, and that each member wear the usual badge of mourning for thirty days.

SEC. 2. Be it further resolved, That the National Secretary is hereby authorized to send a copy of this resolution to the bereaved family of said deceased B. F. Smallwood, and this resolution shall take effect and be in force from and after its passage.

Approved Oct. 14th 1892.

W. N. JONES,
P. C. C. N.

BILL NO. 5.

A resolution authorizing the Senate and House of Representatives to meet in joint session to elect certain officers.

Be it resolved by the General Council of the Choctaw Nation assembled, That the Senate and House of Representatives meet in joint session in the Representative Hall on the 14th day of October 1892, at 10 o'clock A. M. and elect Supreme Judges, Superintendent of Public Schools, and District Trustees.

Further resolved, That this resolution take effect from and after its passage.

Approved Oct., 14th 1892.

W. N. JONES,
P. C. C. N.

BILL NO. 6.

An Act for the relief of Col. C. E. Nelson.

Be it enacted by the General Council of the Choctaw Nation assembled, That the sum of eleven dollars be and is hereby appropriated to pay Col. C. E. Nelson for a Seal furnished by the said C E Nelson for the Circuit Court of the 3d Judicial District of the Choctaw Nation, and the National Auditor is hereby authorized to issue his warrant, and the National Treasurer to pay the same, and this Act shall take effect and be in force from and after its passage.

Approved Oct., 21st 1892.

W. N. JONES,
P. C. C. N.

BILL NO. 7.

An Act removing an election precinct in Cedar County.

Be it enacted by the General Council of the Choctaw Nation assembled. That the election precinct heretofore established at Cedar Creek in Cedar County, known as Cedar Creek precinct, be and the same is hereby removed five miles South west unto Davenport meeting House, and it shall be called and known as Davenport precinct. The election precint of Davenport shall hold its first election at Davenport on the first Wednesday in August 1893, and thereafter this Act; and this Act shall take effect and be in force from and after its passage.

Approved Oct., 21st 1892.

W. N. JONES,
P. C. C. N.

BILL NO. 8.

An Act declaring the last compilation translation and publication of the Choctaw laws from October 1886 and including the Acts of the session of 1890, to be laws of Choctaw Nation in force at the time of their publication.

Whereas on the 31st, day of October 1890 provision was made for the publication of the laws of the Choctaw Nation from the October session of 1886 and including the Acts of the session of 1890, and the Principal Chief was empowered and authorized to appoint compilers, translators and publishers and issue certificates for said work; AND WHEREAS the Principal Chief did appoint such compilers, translators and publishers, and did issue certificates for such work.

Therefore, Be it enacted by the General Council of the Choctaw Nation asssembled, That the said publication is hereby declared to contain the laws of the Choctaw Nation enacted beginning with the Acts, of 1886, and ending with the Acts of 1890, and that they were the laws in force at the said time and respected as such, and this Act shall take effect and be in force from and after its passage.

Approved Oct., 24th 1892.

W. N. JONES,
P. C. C. N.

BILL NO. 9.

An Act authorizing the National Agent to bring suits in the United States Courts against Non-citizens.

Be it enacted by the General Council of the Choctaw Nation assembled, That the National Agent is hereby authorized and empowered to bring suits in the United States Courts against all companies, corporations and individuals, non-citizens operating within the limits of the Choctaw Nation, for royalties of all kinds due the Nation; also for any damage that may befall the Nation through their operations, and that this Act take effect and be in force from and after its passage.

Approved Oct., 24, 1892.

W. N. JONES,
P. C. C N.

BILL NO. 10.

An Act appropriating money for the relief of Edward Spring.

Be it enacted by the General Council of the Choctaw Nation assembled, That the sum of ($71.65) seventy one dollars and sixty-five cents be and is hereby appropriated out of any money in the National Treasury, not otherwise appropriated, to pay Edward Spring for the following items:—taking care of Capitol $50.00; cleaning out the yard $15.00; furnishing two well buckets and two pulleys and ropes $4.10; furnishing four buckets five brooms and six cups $2.55; total $71.65.

And that this Act shall take effect and be in force from and after its passage.

Approved Oct., 25, 1892.

W. N. JONES,
P. C. C. N.

BILL NO. 11

An Act authorizing the District Trustee, Chas. K. Winston to pay certain teachers.

Be it enacted by the General Council of the Choctaw Nation assembled, That Chas. K. Winston, District Trustee of the second District, is hereby authorized to pay out of funds yet in his hands, appropriated last year for school purposes, the sum of ($140.60), one hundred and forty dollars and sixty cents to the following teachers as per accounts viz: J. H. Hufford $40.20; B.

W. Hynes $45.00; Wm. Hamberges; $40.40; Henry Hudson $15.

This Act shall take effect and be in force from and after its passage.

Approved Oct. 26th 1892.

W. N. JONES,
P. C. C. N.

BILL NO. 12.

An Act removing an election precinct of Eagle County.

Be it enacted by the General Council of the Choctaw Nation assembled, That Bohanan precinct in Eagle County is hereby removed three miles East to East Eagle town and it shall be called and known as Eagle town precinct. The election precinct of Eagle town shall hold its first election at East Eagle town on the first Wednesday in August 1893. And all the citizens of Eagle county are privileged to vote at said precinct in all elections.

This Act shall take effect and be in force from and after its passage.

Approved Oct. 25th 1892.

W. N. JONES,
P. C. C. N.

BILL NO. 13.

A resolution accepting the report of Chas. K. Winston District Trustee of the second District.

We, your committee on schools, to whom was referred the report of Chas. K. Winston, District Trustee second District, find the same to be true and correct with a balance on hand of $14,311.20 and ask the adoption of the following resolution to wit:

Be it resolved by the General Council of the Choctaw Nation assembled, That the report of Chas. K. Winston District Trustee of Second District be, and the same is hereby accepted as being true and correct with the balance on hand amounting to $14,311.20, and that this resolution shall take effect and be in force from and after its passage.

Approved Oct 25th 1892.

W. N. JONES,
P. C. C. N.

BILL NO. 14.

A resolution providing for commissioners to meet a similar commission from the Chickasaw Nation.

SECTION, 1. Be it resolved by the General Council of the Choctaw Nation assembled, That the Principal Chief of the Choctaw Nation is hereby authorized and empowered to appoint a Commission of three; one from each District, to meet and confer with a similar Commission from the Chickasaw Nation to settle financial differences between the two Nations.

SEC. 2 Be it further resolved that said Commissioners receive as compensation the sum of five dollars per day, and ten cents per mile each way, while attending t said business, on the certificate of the Principal Chief of the Choctaw Nation; then the Auditor shall issue their warrants, and the Treasurer shall pay the same; also said Commissioners shall make out a full report of their work, as a Commission, to the next regular term of the General Council in Oct. 1893.

SEC. 3. Be it further resolved that this resolution shall take effect and be in force from and after its passage.

Approved Oct. 26th 1892.

W. N. JONES,
P. C. C. N.

BILL NO. 15.

An Act appropriating $8,000.00 for the relief of the Militia.

Be it enacted by the General Council of the Choctaw Nation assembled, That the sum of $8,000.00 eight thousand dollars be and the same is hereby appropriated out of any money in the Treasury not otherwise appropriated, for the relief of the Militia called out by the order of W. N. Jones Principal Chief of the Choctaw Nation, during our late trouble that occurred in September and October 1892. After all Militiamen are compensated, should there be a balance, it shall be returned to the National Treasury.

The National Auditor is hereby directed to issue his warrants for the same on certificate of the Principal Chief and the

National Treasury to pay the same, This Act shall take effect and be in force from and after its passage.

Approved Oct. 26th 1892.

W. N. Jones,
P. C. C. N.

BILL NO. 16.

A resolution appointing a Committee to investigate the claim of General Albert Pike, deceased, against the Choctaw Nation.

Be it resolved by the General Council of the Choctaw Nation assembled, That a special committee consisting of six members from the House and five from the Senate, be and is hereby appointed to investigate the claim of General Albert Pike, deceased, against the Choctaw Nation.

Be it further resolved that the said committee be empowered to summon any person that may know anything in regard to said claim, and that this resolution shall take effect and be in force from and after its passage.

Approved Oct. 26th 1892.

W. N. Jones,
P. C. C. N.

BILL NO. 17.

An Act appropriating money for the relief of Mrs. J. H. Moore.

Be it enacted by the General Council of the Choctaw Nation assembled, That the sum of five hundred dollars is hereby appropriated out of any money in the Treasury, not otherwise appropriated to pay Mrs. J. H. Moore the widow of the late Dr. J. H. Moore for services rendered the Nation in transcribing and preserving the proceedings of the Board of Court of claims from 1876 to 1889.

The National Auditor is hereby required to issue his warrant on the National Treasurer for the same. The said Mrs. J. H. Moore shall accept the five hundred dollars appropriated to be full payment of all claims She may have against the Nation for the services of Dr. J. H. Moore.

This Act to take effect and be in force from and after its passage.

Arpproved this 27th day of Oct. 1892.

W. N. Jones,
P. C. C. N.

BILL NO. 18.

An Act relating to the National Agent's office.

SECTION 1. Be it enacted by the General Council of the Choctaw Nation assembled, That the National Agent shall be permitted to make contract with non-citizens to manufacture, handle or ship timber of all kinds within the limits of the Choctaw Nation, excepting railroad ties. Before contracting with non-citizens, however, the National Agent shall require them to enter into good and sufficient bond in the sum of Ten Thousand Dollars, payable to the United States, to be approved by the Principal Chief of the Choctaw Nation, and conditioned upon their faithful compliance with their contracts; and no non-citizens shall engage in any business contemplated by this Act, except a contract be first made with the National Agent, and a permit be also obtained according to the laws of the Choctaw Nation.

SEC. 2. Be it further enacted, that all parties, whether citizens or non-citizens, operating under a timber contract, made with the National Agent, shall be actual owners of the mills, or other enterprises, and shall not be allowed to sublet, or to include mills, or other enterprises, other than are specified in the contract.

SEC. 3. Be it further enacted, that it shall be unlawful for the Railroad companies to receive for shipment, or to ship any timber other than railroad ties, unless the person desiring to ship, shall first present to their agent a passport, having on it the signature and seal of the National Agent, to show that the royalty has been paid on said timber, and said passport shall be held by the Railroad Agent until called in by the National Agent, which shall be done at the end of each fiscal quarter. All railroad companies not complying with the provisions of this Act shall be held responsible for the royalties due the Nation on the timber shipped.

SEC. 4. Be it further enacted, that all monies collected by the National Agent through the United States Courts, shall be paid direct to the Treasurer of the Choctaw Nation.

SEC. Be it further enacted that all Acts or parts of Acts

coming in conflict with the provisions of this Act are hereby repealed, and that

This Act shall take effect and be in force from and after its passage.

Approved Oct. 27th 1892.

W. N. JONES,
P. C. C. N.

BILL NO. 19.

A resolution of adjournment.

Be it resolved by the General Council of the Choctaw Nation assembled, That the present session of the General Council adjourn Friday, at 12 o'clock A. M., November 4th, 1892, and that this resolution shall take effect and be in force from and after its passage.

Approved Oct 28th 1892.

W. N. JONES,
P. C. C. N.

BILL NO. 20.

An Act establishing an election precinct in Cedar County.

SECTION 1. Be it enacted by the General Council of the Choctaw Nation assembled, That an election precinct is hereby established at or near the Gilbert Cooper place in Cedar County to be called and hereafter known as Lick Precinct.

SEC. 2. Be it further enacted, that the first election held at said Lick Precinct, shall be on the first Wednesday in August, 1893, and thereafter; and this Act shall take effect and be in force from and after its passage.

Approved Oct. 28th 1892.

W. N. JONES,
P. C. C. N.

BILL NO. 21.

An Act amendatory of an Act establishing the time of meeting of the Circuit Court of the 1st District.

Be it enacted by the General Council of the Choctaw Nation assembled, That Section 3rd of an Act establishing the time of meeting of the Circuit Court of the First District, approved Nov. 6th, 1883, is hereby amended so that said court shall meet on the second Monday in November of each year instead of on the first.

All Acts or parts of Acts coming in conflict with this Act are hereby repealed, and this Act shall take effect and be in force from and after its passage.

Approved Oct. 12th 1892.

W. N. JONES,
P. C. C. N.

BILL NO. 22

An Act amendatory of the law against hunting on Sunday.

Be it enacted by the General Council of the Choctaw Nation assembled, That the law against hunting on Sunday, passed and approved Oct. 17, 1883, be so amended to read.

SECTION 1. It shall not be lawful for any person to carry a gun or to hunt with a dog or gun on Sunday in the Choctaw Nation.

SEC. 2. Be it further amended that the fine for the said violation shall be from Ten to Twenty-Five Dollars.

SEC. 3. Be it further enacted that all Acts and parts of Acts coming in conflict with these amendments are hereby repealed, and this Act take effect and be in force from and after its passage.

Approved Oct., 28th 1892.

W. N. JONES,
P. C. C. N.

BILL NO. 23.

An Act establishing the Militia Law.

We, your committee on Chief's Message, recommend the following enactment:

Be it enacted by the General Council of the Choctaw Nation assembled, That the law passed and approved Nov. 28, 1888, suspending the Militia Law be, and the same is hereby repealed, and the Militia Law declared in full force and effect from and after the passage of this Act.

Approved Oct., 28th, 1892.

W. N. JONES,
P. C. C N.

BILL NO. 24.

A resolution adopting the report of Amos Henry, District Trustee of the First District, C. N.

To THE GENERAL COUNCIL:—Your committee on schools, report after having examined the report of Amos Henry, District Trustee of the 1st District, carefully and impartially find the same to be true and correct with a balance on hand amounting to $10,464.40 and we respectfully ask the adoption of the following resolution.

Be it resolved by the General Council of the Choctaw Nation assembled, That the report of Amos Henry, District Trustee 1st District, C. N., be, and the same is hereby accepted as being true and correct, and this resolution shall take affect and be in force from and after its passage.

Approved Oct., 28th, 1892.

W. N. JONES,
P. C. C. N.

BILL NO. 25.

A resolution adopting the report of T. B. Turnbull, District Trustee 3rd District.

To THE GENERAL COUNCIL:—Your committee on schools, after having examined the report of T. B. Turnbull, District Trustee of the 3rd District, carefully and impartially find the same to be true and correct with a balance on hand amounting to $15,293.60, and we respectfully ask the adoption of the following resolution:

Be it resolved by the General Council of the Choctaw Nation assembled, That the report of T. B. Turnbull, District Trustee of 3rd District, C. N., be, and the same is hereby accepted as true and correct and this resolution shall take effect and be in force from and after its passage.

Approved Oct., 31st 1892.

W. N. JONES,
P. C. C. N

BILL NO. 26.

A resolution adopting the report of R. C. Robe, Superintendent of Wheelock Seminary.

To THE GENERAL COUNCIL:—Your committee on schools, after having examined the report of R. C. Robe, Superintendent of Wheelock Seminary, find the same to be true and correct and ask the passage of the following resolution.

Be it resolved by the General Council of the Choctaw Nation assembled, That the report of R. C. Robe, Superintendent of Wheelock Seminary, be, and the same is hereby accepted as being true and correct, and this resolution shall take effect and be in force from and after its passage.

Approved Oct. 31st, 1892.

W. N. JONES,
P. C. C. N.

BILL NO. 27.

An Act for the relief of Isaac Brown, Deputy Sheriff of Wade County.

Be it enacted by the General Council of the Choctaw Nation assembled, That the sum of one hundred and fifty dollars is hereby appropriated out of any money in the treasury not otherwise appropriated, to pay Isaac Brown the expenses of a law suit, caused by trouble brought on by the enforcing of our law while acting as a Deputy Sheriff of Wade County. The National Auditor is hereby requested to issue his warrant on the National Treasurer for the said amount.

This Act to take effect and be in force from and after its passage.

Approved Oct. 31st, 1892.

W. N. JONES,
P. C. C. N.

BILL NO. 28.

An Act granting G. W. Thompson and G. W. Dukes the privilege to establish a toll gate

Be it enacted by the General Council of the Choctaw Nation assembled, That the privilege is hereby granted to G. W. Thompson and G. W. Dukes to establish a toll gate on the road leading up to the Mineral Spring on Sugar Loaf Mountain upon the following conditions: If the said Thompson and Dukes shall by grading the earth and removing the rocks, make a good traveled road or highway from the foot of Sugar Loaf Mountain up to the Mineral Spring, a distance of three miles, they shall be entitled to demand and receive toll from all persons, except citizens, passing over said road as follows: For each four horse or ox wagon, fifty cents; drawn by two animals, twenty-five cents; by one horse, ten cents; man on horse back, ten cents; stock in heard, one cent each. Said toll may be collected as soon as the road is in good condition and continue ten years or so long as the road is kept in good condition, and this Act shall take effect and be in force from and after its passage

Approved Nov. 2nd, 1892.

W. N. JONES,
P. C. C. N.

BILL NO. 29.

An Act providing for settlement of royalty due on the construction of the Choctaw Coal and Railway Co.'s Railroad.

SECTION 1. Be it enacted by the General Council of the Choctaw Nation assemblad, That there is due the Choctaw Nation the sum of nine thousand two hundred and twenty-seven dollars ($9,227.00) as royalty on timber used in constructing said Choctaw Coal and Railway Co's road, and the National Agent is hereby authorized to bring the necessary suits or suit against any person or corporation to procure the payment of said royalty to the Choctaw Nation, and to pay to attorneys a conditional fee of 10 per cent, of whatever amount may be recovered.

SEC 2. The inspectors on said railroad shall not be entitled to 10 per cent. of this money, not having rendered any service therein, and this Act shall take effect and be in force from and after its passage.

Approved Nov. 3rd, 1892.

W. N. JONES,
P. C. C. N.

BILL NO. 30.

A resolution adopting the report of W. A. Caldwell, Superintendent of Spencer Academy.

We your committee on schools, to whom was referred the report of W. A. Caldwell, Superintendent of Spencer Academy have thoroughly examined the same and find it to be true and correct with no balance on hand and ask the adoption of the following resolution.

Be it resolved by the General Council of the Choctaw Nation assembled, That the report of W. A. Caldwell, Superintendent of Spencer Academy, be, and the same is hereby accepted as being true and correct, and this resolution shall take effect and be in force from and after its passage.

Approved Nov. 3rd, 1892.

W. N. JONES,
P. C. C. N.

BILL NO. 31.

An Act to grant a right of way for a coal railway branch or switch to G. W. Dukes, R. J. Ward, W. N. Jones and W J. Kayser.

SECTION 1. Be it enacted by the General Council of the Choctaw Nation assembled, That a right of way of one hundred feet in width is hereby granted to G. W. Dukes, R. J. Ward, W. N. Jones and W. J. Kayser, to construct and operate a branch or switch railroad, making a junction with the St. Louis and San Francisco Ry., at or near Cameron Station, on said railroad in Skullyville County, Choctaw Nation, and running thence in a west by northwest direction, a distance of four or five miles to coal veins or mines which have been leased to S. J. Wright, of Paris, Texas, and his associates, with branches to reach the several veins or mines aforesaid, with the right to it or its assigns to use timber, stone and dirt, to construct and maintain and operate such tracks. branches, sidings, extensions, telegraph and telephone lines as may be necessary along and upon the right of way herein granted.

SEC. 2. The right of way terminal at the said coal mines and the station connections with the St. Louis and San Francisco Railway at or near Cameron Station, may be enlarged in addition to the right of way to a width of three hundred feet by two thousand feet in length for depot purposes to facilitate the handling and shipping of coal. This grant shall not authorize the entrance or intrusion upon any citizens claims, without his or her consent and shall not be construed to convey the land in fee or to grant any more rights than to occupy the land while coal is being transported to market over it, and it shall cease and revert to the Choctaw Nation whenever it is abandoned or whenever the transportation of coal over it is discontinued.

SEC. 3. If the construction of this branch railroad herein

provided for, shall not have been entered upon in two years after the grant, it shall be void, and this Act shall take effect and be in force from and af er its passa e.

Approved Nov 3rd, 1892.

W. N. JONES,
P. C. C. N.

BILL NO. 32.

A resolution accepting the report of Dr. A. Griffith, Superintendent of New Hope Seminary, C. N.

We your committe on schools, to whom was referred the report of Dr. A. Griffith, Superintendent of New Hope Seminary, C. N., have examined the same, and find it to be true and correct with a balance on hand amounting to nineteen dollars and eighty-five cents ($19.85) and ask the adoption of the following resolution, to-wit:

Be it resolved by the General Council of the Choctaw Nation assembled, That the report of Dr. A. Grifflth, Superintendent of New Hope Seminary, be, and the same is hereby accepted as being true and correct, and this resolution shall take effect and be in force from and after its passage

Approved Nov 4th, 1892.

W. N. JONFS,
P. C. C. N.

BILL NO 33.

An Act for the relief of H. T. Jackman.

Be it enacted by the General Council of the Choctaw Nation assembled, That the sum of ($103.50) one hundred and three dollars and fifty cents be, and the same is hereby appropriated out of any mon-y in the treasury not otherwise appropriated to pay H. T. Jackman for digging and walling a well for capitol, $100.00; also to six window lights, $21.00; putting in the same $2.50; to al, $103.50.

The National Auditor is hereby authorized to issue his warrant for said am unt and the National Treasurer shall pay the same, and this Act shall take effect and be in force from and after its passage

Approved Nov. 4th, 1892.

W. N. JONES,
P. C. C. N.

BILL NO. 34.

A resolution accepting the report of C. J. Rallston: Superintendent of Armstrong Orphan Academy, C. N.

We, your committee on schools, to whom was referred the report of C. J. Rallston, Superintendent of Armstrong Academy, C. N., have examined the same and find it to be true and correct with a balance on hand amounting to two dollars and forty five cents ($2 45) and ask the adoption of the following resolution, to-wit:

Be it resolved by the General Council of the Choctaw Nation assembled, That the report of C. J. Rallston, Superintendant of Armstrong Academy, be, and the same is hereby accepted as being true and correct, and that this resolution take effect and be in force from and after its passage.

Approved Nov. 4th, 1892.

W. N. Jones,
P. C. C. N.

BILL NO. 35.

An Act legalizing certain Acts heretofore approved by the President of the Senate.

Be it enacted by the General Council of the Choctaw Nation assembled, That all of those Acts establishing election precints, which were approved by the President of the Senate, when acting as Principal Chief of the Choctaw Nation in the absence of the Principal Chief, and which were declared by the Supreme Court unconstitutional and have not been repealed, are hereby legalized, and all of said election precints are hereby established, and this Act shall take effect and be in force from and after its passage.

Approved Nov. 4th 1892.

W. N. Jones,
P. C. C. N.

BILL NO. 36

An Act making appropriation for students in the states.

Section 1. Be it enacted by the General Council of the Choctaw Nation assembled, That the sum of Twelve Thousand Five Hundred Dollars is hereby appropriated to defray the expenses of forty students attending schools in the states—twenty boys and twenty girls—to be expended in proportion of Three Hundred Dollars each for boys, and Three Hundred and Twenty-Five Dollars for each girl.

SEC. 2. That this Act take effect and be in force from and after its passage.

Approved Nov., 4th 1892.

W. N. JONES,
P. C. C. N.

BILL NO. 37.

An Act making appropriation for the relief of J. J. Gardner.

Your committee to whom was referred the petition of J. J. Gardner, asking for appropriation to enable him to defend the rights of jurisdiction of the Choctaw Nation in his case pending before the United States Court at Paris, Texas, have had the same under consideration and report the following Act and ask its passage.

Be it enacted by the General Council of the Choctaw Nation assembled, That the sum of Five Hundred Dollars be and is hereby appropriated out of any money in the National Treasury not otherwise appropriated, to enable J. J. Gardner to employ attorneys to defend his case, pending in the United States court at Paris, Texas. On the certificate of the Principal Chief the Auditor shall issue this warrant for the amount.

Be it further enacted, That this Act shall take effect and be in force from and after its passage.

Approved Nov. 4th 1892.

W. N. JONES,
P. C. C N.

BILL NO. 38.

TO THE GENERAL COUNCIL:—

Under the contract between the Board of Education of the Choctaw Nation and Dukes & Ryan there is a balance due them of one hundred and eighty-five dollars, to be provided for by appropriation of the General Council. We therefore recommend that the above amount be provided in order to complete said contract. Recommended by Board of Education.

Therefore, be it enacted by the General Council of the

Choctaw Nation assembled, That the sum of One Hundred and Eighty-Five Dollars, is hereby appropriated out of any money in the Treasury not otherwise appropriated, to pay G. W. Dukes and Ryan on account of above balance and this Act shall take effect and be in force from and after its passage.

Approved Nov. 4th 1892.

W. N. JONES,
P. C. C. N.

BILL NO. 39.

An Act recognizing the citizenship of Tom York, Charley York; Sampson York, Lee Silman and their families, late arrivals from Mississippi,

Be it resolved by the General Council of the Choctaw Nation assembled, That Tom York and his wife, Charley York and four children, Sampson York, wife and two children, and Lee Silman, late arrivals from the state of Mississippi are hereby recognized as Choctaws; and entitled to all rights, privileges and immunities of other Choctaws by blood, and this Act shall take effect and be in force from and after its passage.

Appproved November 4th 1892.

W. N. JONES,
P. C. C. N.

BILL NO. 40.

An Act appropriating $120.00 for the relief of Tom York and others herein named.

SECTION 1. Be it enacted by the General Council of the Choctaw Nation assembled. That the sum of $120.00 is hereby appropriated out of any money in the Treasury not otherwise appropriated, for the relief of Tom York and his wife, Charley York and four children, Sampson York, wife and two children, and Lee Silman who are late arrivals from Mississippi and are in need: said sum of $120.00 to be divided equally among the said late arrivals.

SEC. 2. Be it further enacted that this Act take effect and be in force from and after its passage.

Approved Nov. 4, 1892.

W. N JONES,
P. C. C. N.

BILL NO. 41.

A resolution respecting the report of S. T. Dwight and J. P. Turnbull.

Your Committee on Schools report that S. T. Dwight and J. P. Turnbull each of whom were Supt., of Schools a part of the past year, and neither have sent in their report. We therefore recommend the passage of the following resolution.

Be it resolved by the General Council of the Choctaw Nation assembled, That S. T. Dwight and J. P. Turnbull are hereby requested to each send in their report for past years service to the next session of the General Council of the Choctaw Nation.

This resolution shall take effect and be in force from and after its passage.

Approved Nov. 4, 1892.

W. N. JONES,
P. C. C. N.

BILL NO. 42.

An Act regulating the granting of certificates to teachers of neighborhood schools.

SECTION 1. Be it resolved by the General Council of the Choctaw Nation assembled, That for ascertaining the qualifications of Teachers in the Neighborhood schools, the applicant shall pay to the person conducting the examination the sum of two and 50-100 dollars—Provided citizens shall not be required to pay any thing.

SEC. 2. All Acts in conflict with this Act are hereby repealed and this Act shall take effect and be in force from and after its passage.

Approved Nov. 4, 1892.

W. N. JONES,
P. C. C. N.

BILL NO. 43.

An Act Making appropriation for the fiscal year ending July 31, 1893.

SECTION I. Be it enacted by the General Council of the Choctaw Nation assembled, That the following sums of money are hereby appropriated for the general expenses of the Choctaw Nation during the fiscal year ending July 31, 1893, to-wit:

Principal Chief	$ 2000 00
Treasurer, Auditor and Secretary	1800 00
National Agent	800 00
" Attorney	400 00
Private Secretary	500 00
National Lighthorsemen	2450 00
Supreme Judges	1200 00
Circuit "	1500 00
County "	4250 00
District Chief	150 00
" Attorneys	950 00
Election Judges and Clerks	680 00
Grand and Petit Juries	14900 00
Witness Fees Attending Circuit Court	6000 00
Superintendent of schools and trustees	1800 00
Contingent fund for Chief	400 00
" " " Superintendent	650 00
" " " District Trustees	750 00
" " " Auditor	400 00
" " " Treasurer	400 00
" " " Secretary	400 00
Publication Fund	350 00
Clerk Supreme Court	100 00
" County courts	1700 00
" Circuit "	900 00
Sheriffs	5100 00
Rangers	850 00
Sheriffs and deputies attending Circuit Court	1850 00
Deputy Sheriffs	6800 00
Sheriff Attending Supreme Court	50 00
Care of Capital	50 00
General Council and Light-horsemen and Clerk Citiship	9200 00
Students in States	12500 00
First District Neighborhood Schools 2nd " " " 3rd " " "	42000 00
Spencer Academy	10000 00
New Hope Seminary	10000 00
Armstrong Orphan Home	7000 00
Wheelock Seminary	5600 00
Jones' Academy	10000 00
Tushka Humma Female Institute	10000 00
Tushka Lusa Institute	3000 00

Teachers and employes of Jones Academy, New Hope Seminary and Tushka Humma F Institute	5850 00
Salary Sup't Jones Academy, New Hope Seminary, and T. F. Institute - - - - -	3600 00
Election judges for 1891 - - - - -	408 00
Examining Board (Proxies) - - - - -	810 00
Officers pro tem for 1892 and 1893 - -	200 00
Mileage for Supreme Judges (Including 1891) -	200 00
Outstanding Local Trustees Certificates - -	100 00
Supreme Court expenses for Stationary, allowed by Supreme Court - - - - - - -	25 00

Approved Nov., 4th 1892.

W. N. JONES,
P. C. C. N.

---o---

I HEREBY CERTIFY, That the foregoing Acts snd Resolutions, are true and correct copies taken from the originals now on file in my office.

In witness whereof I have hereto set my hand and affixed the seal of the Choctaw Nation, this 7th day of February, A. D. 1893.

[SEAL.]

J. B. JACKSON,
National Secretary, Choctaw Nation.

INDEX.

	PAGE
Adjournment, Resolution of	12
Appropriation for fiscal year	22
Bohannon, Ellis—relief of	3
Brown, Isaac—relief of	15
Certificates—granting of	22
Citizenship—Tom York, et al.,	21
Cedar County—election precinct	6
Commission to meet Chickasaws	9
Ceder County—election precinct	12
Circuit Court—time of meeting	12
Caldwell, W. A. Report of	16
Dukes & Ryan. Relief of	20
Dwight, S. T. Report of	22
Eagle County. Removal of Pre	8
Griffith, A. Report of	18
Gardner, J. J. Relief of	20
Hunting on Sunday	13
Henry, Amos—Report of	14
Joint Session—both houses	5
Jackman, H. T. Relief of	18
Lighthorsemen—Increasing salary of	4
Laws—accepting compilation	6
Legalizing Acts signed by President Senate	19
Militia—Relief of	9
Moore, J. H, Relief of	10

	PAGE
Militia Laws—relation to	13
Nelson, C. E. Relief of	5
National Agent—Relating to	11
Pike—claim of—investigation	10
Robe, R. C. Report of	14
Royalty—on Choctaw road	16
Right of Way—granting	17
Rallston, C. J. Report of	19
Smallwood, B. F. Resolutions of respect to	4
Suits vs. Non-citizens—respect to	7
Spring—relief of	7
Students in States	19
Turnbull, T. B. Report of	14
Toll Gate—right of	15
Votes—Respect to counting	3
Winston, C. K. Respect to	7
Winston, C. K. Report of	8
York, Tom—relief of	21

LAWS

—OF THE—

Choctaw Nation

—PASSED AT THE—

Regular Session of the General Council

—CONVENED AT—

TUSHKA HOMMA,

Oct. 2, 1893, and Adjourned Oct. 27, 1893,

—AND THE—

SPECIAL SESSIONS

CONVENED IN FEBRUARY 1892

—AND—

CONVENED IN JUNE, 1893.

ATOKA, IND. TER.
INDIAN CITIZEN PUBLISHING CO.
1894.

LAWS OF THE

CHOCTAW NATION, REGULAR SESSION.

1893.

BILL NO. 1.

An act conferring citizenship on certain persons named.

Be it enacted by the General Council of the Choctaw Nation assembled, That Abbot Leflore, Felicia Landors, Louis C. Leflore and his three children, Rosa, Michael and Josephine, late of the State of Mississippi; are hereby recognized as citizens of the Choctaw Nation, and entitled to all the rights, privileges and immunities of citizens of this Nation, and this act shall take effect and be in force from and after its passage.

Approved Oct. 13, 1893.

W. N. JONES,
P. C. C. N.

BILL NO. 2.

A resolution showing the financial settlement of the Choctaw Nation with J. W. Ownby.

We your committee on finance to whom the account of J. W. Ownby was referred, have examined the same and find that he has compromised with the committee on Chiefs Message of Special Session of Council of June 1893, for $3000 and that this amount has been settled with the said J. W. Ownby. Therefore be it

Resolved, By the General Council of the Choctaw Nation assembled; That the additional compensation asked for be, and the same is hereby rejected, and that this resolution take effect and be in force from and after its passage.

Approved Oct. 13, 1893.

W. N. JONES,
P. C. C. N.

BILL NO. 3.

An act extending Toll Bridge privileges over Perryville Creek, granted Oct, 31st, 1872 to Oct. 31st, 1902.

SECTION 1. Be it enacted by the General Council of the Choctaw Nation assembled, That an act granting a toll bridge over Perryville Creek to James S. Johnson from Oct. 31, 1872 to Oct. 31, 1882, and subsequently renewed to Oct. 31, 1892, be and the same is hereby further renewed so as to extend to Oct. 31, 1902, to Annie Keys, formerly wife of and now legal heir of the said James S. Johnson in accordance with the conditions of the grant of Oct. 31, 1872.

SEC. 2. Be it further enacted that in addition to the privileges of the grant of Oct. 31, 1872, the said Annie Keys shall have exclusive bridge privileges one mile in both directions up and down the stream from the said bridge, provided she does not interfere with former settlers, and this act to take effect and be in force from and after its passage.

Approved Oct. 16, 1893.

W. N. JONES,
P. C. C. N.

BILL NO. 4.

A resolution accepting the report of S. T. Dwight, Superintendent of Jones Academy.

We, your committee on schools to whom was referred the report of S. T. Dwight, superintendent of Jones Academy, have thoroughly examined the same and find it to be true and correct, with no balance on hand and ask the adoption of the following resolution, to-wit:

Be it resolved, by the General Council of the Choctaw Nation assembled, That the report of S. T. Dwight, superintendent of Jones Academy be and the same is hereby accepted as being true and correct, and this resolution shall take effect and be in force from and after its passage.

Approveed Oct. 16. 1893.

W. N. JONES,
P. C. C. N.

BILL NO. 5.

A resolution accepting the report of W. A. Caldwell, Superitendent of Spencer Academy.

We, your committee on schools, to whom was referred the report of W. A. Caldwell, superintendeat of Spencer Academy, have thoroughly examined the same and find it to be true and correct, with a balance on hand of two dollars and thirteen cents ($2. 13), and ask the adoption of this resolution, to-wit:

Be it resolved, by the General Council of the Choctaw Nation assembled, That the report of W. A. Caldwell, superintendent of Spencer Academy, be and the same is hereby accepted as being true and correct, and this resolution shall take effect and be in force from and after its passage.

Approved Oct. 16, 1893

W. N: JONES.
P. C. C. N.

BILL NO. 6.

A resolution accepting the report of Amos Henry, District Trustee of the First District.

We, your committee on schools, to whom was referred the report of Amos Henry, District Trustee of the First District, have examined the same and find it to be correct and true, with a balance on hand of two thousand one hundred and eighty-seven dollars and forty cents (2,187. 40), and ask the adoption of the following resolution, to-wit:

Be it resolved by the General Council of the Choctaw Nation assembled, That the report of Amos Henry, District Trustee of the First District, be and the same is hereby accepted as being true and correct, with a balance on hand of two thousand one hundred and eighty-seven dollars and forty cents (2,187.40) and this resolution shall take effect and be in force from and after its passage.

Approved Oct. 18. 1893.

W. N. JONES,
P. C. C. N.

BILL NO. 7.

A resolution accepting the report of D. A. Riddle; District Trustee of the 3rd District.

We, your committee on schools, to whom was referred the report of D. A. Riddle, District Trustee, have examined the same and find it be true and correct, with a balance on hand of four hundred and sixty-seven dollars and eighty cents (467. 80) and ask the adoption of the following resolution, to-wit:

Be it resolved by the General Council of the Choctaw Nation assembled, That the report of D. A. Riddle, District Trustee of the Third District, be and the same is hereby accepted as being true and correct, with a balance on hand ot four hundred and sixty-seven dollars and eighty cents (467. 80), and this resolution shall take effect and be in force fr m and after its passage.

Approved Oct. 18, 1893.

W. N. JONES,
P. C. C. N.

BILL NO. 8.

A resolution accepting the report of Ed Wilson. District Trustee of the 2nd District.

We, your committee, to whom was referred the report of Ed Wilson, District Trustee of the Second District, have thoroughly examined the same and find it to be true and correct, with a balance on hand of four hundred and fifty dollars and fifty-five cents ($450. 55), and ask the adoption of the following resolution, to-wit:

Be it resolved by the General Council of the Choctaw Nation assembled, That the report of Ed Wilson, District Trustee of the Second District, be and the same is hereby accepted as true and correct, with a balance on hand of four hundred and fifty dollars and fifty-five cents ($450. 55), and this resolution shall take effect and be in force from and after its passage.

Approved Oct. 18, 1893.

W. N. JONES,
P. C. C. N.

BILL NO. 9.

An act for the relief of J. S. Standley.

SECTION 1. Be it enacted by the General Council of the

Choctaw Nation assembled, That the sum of three hundred dollars ($300) be and the same is hereby appropriated, out of any money in the National Treasury, not otherwise appropriated, to pay J. S. Standley for services rendered in recovering the interest on Light-Horse fund; said three hundred dollars being ten per cent of total amount recovered.

SEC. 2. Be it further enacted that the National Auditor is hereby ordered to issue his warrant upon the National Treasurer for the sum, and this act to take effect and be in force from and after its passage.

Approved Oct. 19, 1893.

W. N. JONES,
P. C. C. N.

BILL NO. 10.

A resolution authorizing the National Secretary to sell certain law books.

Be it enacted by the General Council of the Choctaw Nation assembled, That the National Secretary be and is hereby authorized to sell the balance of the law books in his office that were published in the year 1891, containing the acts of 1886 to 1891 inclusive, price to be two dollars each.

Be it further enacted, That the National Secretary shall turn the proceeds of the sales of the law books to the National Treasurer, and take his receipts for the amount turned over, and report the sales of the law books to the next session of the General Council, and this resolution shall take effect from and after its passage.

Approved Oct. 19, 1893

W. N JONES,
P. C. C. N.

BILL NO. 11.

An act repealing an act passed and approved June 29, 1893, locating the Circuit Court Ground of Mosholotubbee District in Gaines County.

Be it enacted by the General Council of the Choctaw Nation assembled, That an act passed June 29, 1893, be and the same is hereby repealed, and the following is hereby substituted:

The Circuit Court Ground of Mosholotubbee district in Gaines county, is hereby removed to one mile southwest of the said James Brown place, and shall be called and known as Hoc-hubbee Court Ground. The district court of Masholotubbee district shall hold its first session at Mocholubbee Court Ground on the 2nd Monday of November 1893, and all courts, special and general shall henceforth be held there; and all acts or parts of acts coming in conflict with the provisions of this act are hereby repealed, and this act shall take effect and be in force from and after its passage.

Approved Oct. 19, 1893.

W. N. Jones,
P. C. C. N.

BILL NO. 12.

An act creating the office of delegate to the Congress of the United States, prescribing his duties, and providing for his compensation.

Be it enacted by the General Council of the Choctaw Nation assembled,

Section 1. That the office of delegate to the Congress of the United States be and the same is hereby created; that said delegate so appointed as herein provided shall be not less than thirty-five years of age, and a Choctaw Indian by blood.

Sec. 2. That said delegate shall be appointed by the Principal Chief, by and with the consent and approval of the senate; said delegate shall represent the Choctaw Nation in all her interests whatsoever in congress, and before the departments, and shall keep the Principal Chief thoroughly advised as to all matters under his charge and supervision, and he shall make an annual report of all matters in his charge to the General Council, and such further and other reports as he may be called upon to make from time to time by the Principal Chief.

Sec. 3. That the term of office of said delegate shall be for four years. He shall be required to reside at Washington, D. C., and shall be present during all sessions of congress, unless otherwise ordered or directed by the Principal Chief.

Sec. 4. That the salary of said delegate shall be five thousand ($5000) dollars per annum payable quarterly upon warrants to be issued by the National Auditor. The first quarter allowance of said delegate to be paid in advance at the time of his appointment.

SEC. 5. That said delegate is authorized and empowered to employ such attorney or attorneys as he may deem advisable and by and with the advice and consent of the Principal Chief, on requisition drawn by said delegate and countersigned by the Principal Chief, on the treasurer of the Choctaw Nation to disburse and expend not more than two thausand ($2009) dollars per annum in payment of such attorney or attorneys so employed by said delegate,

SEC. 6. That this act shall take effect and be in force from and after its passage.

Approved Oct. 19, 1893.

W. N. JONES,
P. C. C. N.

BILL NO. 13.

A reoolution accepting the report of Dr. C. H. Ellis, Superintendent of Wheelock Seminery.

We, your committee on schools, to whom was referred the report of Dr. C. H. Ellis, Superintendent of Wheelock Seminary, have thoroughbly examined the same and find it to be true and correct, with no balance on hand, and would ask the adoption of the following resolution to-wit:

Be it resolved by the General Council of the Choctaw Nation assembled, That the report of Dr. C. H. Ellis, Superintendent of Wheelock Seminary be and the same is hereby accepted as true and correct, and this resolution shall take effect and be in force from and after its passage.

Approved Oct. 19, 1893.

W. N. JONES,
P. C. C. N.

BILL NO. 14.

An act prohibiting the floating of timber from the Choctaw Nation.

SECTION 1. Be it enacted by the General Council of the Choctaw Nation assembled. That the rafting or floating of timber, or an attempt to raft or float timber of all kinds within the limits of the Choctaw Nation, or from the Choctaw Nation, shall be prohibited after January 31st, 1894.

SEC. 2. That any person or persons violating the provisions of this act after the above named date shall thereby forfeit his or their contract and the National Agent shall revoke the same.

SEC. 3. That the National Secretary is hereby commanded to publish this law for four weeks in the papers of the Choctaw Nation, andn i one paper in Ft. Smith, Ark., and in one paper of Paris, Texas.

SEC, 4. That the sheriffs of all the counties shall advise the National Agent ot parties violating the provisions of this act and this act shall take effect and be in force from and after its passage.

Approved Oct. 19, 1893.

W. N. JONES,
P. C. C. N.

BILL NO. 15.

To the General Council.

Your committee to whom was referred the report of C. S. Vinson, Col. T. D. Ainsworth and G. W. Dukes, commissioners on the part of the Choctaw Nation according to resolution passed Oct. 26, 1892, to meet and confer with a similar commission from the Chickasaw Nation, to settle financial differences between the two Nations, and after having carefully examined the report and agreement of said commissioners, we find that the Chickasaw commissioners failed to comply with their part of said agreement with the Choctaw commissioners, and therefore we cannot recommend said report as a settlement.

SEC. 1. Be it resolved by the General Council of the Choctaw Nation assembled, That the report of the above said commissioners is not accepted as a settlement made between the Choctaw and Chickasaw Nations, and that this resolution take effect and be in force from and after its passage.

Approved Oct. 19, 1894.

W. N. JONES,
P. C. C. N.

BILL NO. 16.

An Act for the relief of G. W. Thompson for taking care of the Capitol building, repainting etc.

Be it enacted by the General Council of the Choctaw Nation assembled, That the sum of two hundred and ten dollars and 90cts ($210.90) be and the sum is hereby appropriated out of any money in the Treasury, not otherwise appropriated to pay G. W. Thompson for services rendered as follows:

Painting Capitol building - - - - -	$90 00
Caring for and scrubbing Capitol building - -	50 00
7 Cords wood - - - - - - -	8 50
2 Gates and hings - - - - - -	1 00
Making steps - - - - - - -	25 00
Rope - - - - - - - -	1 60
10 Gallons Linseed oil - - - - -	9 50
5 Gallons Turpentine . - - - - -	4 50
50 Pounds White Lead - - - - .	7 75
Nails - - - - - - - -	1 25
Well Pully and rope - - - . . .	1 00
Lumber for steps and yard fence - - -	10 80
Total	$210.90.

The National Auditor is hereby authorized to issue his warrant for said amount and the National Treasurer shall pay the same, and this act shall take effect and be in force from and after its passage.

Approved Oct., 19, 1893.

W. N. JONES,
P. C. C. N.

BILL NO. 17.

A resolution accepting the report of Green McCurtain, National Treasurer.

We your committee to whom was referred the report of Green McCurtain, National Treasurer of the Choctaw Nation, find that during the fiscal year ending July 31st 1893, he received and disbursed the following amounts:

RECEIPTS.

Balance from 1891-1892, . - - - - -	$77,541.53
Net Proceeds balance - - - - - - -	22,163.47

U. S. Trust Fund	61,397.85
Osage C and M. Co.	19,172.51
Kansas and Texas C. Co.	1,198.41
Atoka C. and M. Co	17,906.56
South West C. and I. Co.	57,218.03
Choctaw C. and Ry. Co.	20,342.26
Inspectors	18,792.39
Collectors	7,899.12
Sheriffs	95.50
Right of way R. R.	5,554.64
	$284,287.47

EXPENDITURES.

Warrant First Head	10,004,18$\frac{2}{3}$
" 2nd "	6,789,58
" 3rd "	6,650.00
" 4th "	11,500.00
" 5th "	740.00
" 6th "	4,784.90
" " "	5,292.60
" " "	2,024.85
" 7th "	91,351,00
" 8th "	12,645,80
" Weighers "	12,254-13
" Militia "	37,816.20
" Trustees "	66.00
" Judge Protem "	39.50
" School 1st Dist. "	11,800.10
" " 2nd " "	9,496.45.
" " 3rd " "	16,773.30
Total	240,018.67$\frac{2}{3}$

Balance on hand including Net Pro'ceed 44,263,79$\frac{1}{3}$.

And would recommend the passage of the following resolution:

Be it resolved by the General Council of the Choctaw Nation assembled, That the report of Green McCurtain, National Treasurer, for the fiscal year ending July 31st 1893 be and the same is hereby accepted as true and correct.

And this resolution shall take effect from and after its passage.

Approved Oct. 20, 1893.

W. N. JONES,
P. C. C. N.

BILL NO. 18.

An Act abolishing the office of Coal Weighers.

Be it enacted by the General Council of the Choctaw Nation assembled, That the office of National Coal Weighers created by An Act approved Nov. 1st 1882, and amended Oct. 26, 1888 is hereby repealed.

SEC 2. Be it further enacted that this act shall take effect and be in force from and after its passage.

Approved Oct. 20, 1893.

W. N. JONES,
P. C. C. N.

BILL NO. 19.

An Act in relation to the Boarding Schools.

Be it enacted by the General Council of the Choctaw Nation assembled,

SEC. 1. That the requirements necessary for admission into any of the Boarding Schools of the Choctaw Nation shall not include literary qualifications but only such other requirements as the school Board may see fit to impose from time to time.

SEC. 2. That all acts or parts of acts coming in conflict with the provisions of this act be and the same are hereby repealed, and this act to take effect from and after its passage.

Approved Oct. 21, 1893.

W. N. JONES,
P. C. C. N.

BILL NO. 20.

A Resolution of Adjournment.

Be it resolved by the General Council of the Choctaw Nation assembled, That the present session of the General Council of the Choctaw Nation shall adjourn on Friday at 12, o'clock M the 27th day of Oct. 1893, And this resolution shall take effect and be in force from and after its passage.

Approved Oct. 24, 1893.

W. N. JONES,
P. C. C. N.

BILL NO. 21.

A resolution accepting the report of Wallace Bond District Collector.

Your Committee to whom was referred the report of Wallace Bond District Collector of the first District, have carefully examined the same, and find it to be true and correct, and ask the adoption of the following resolution:

Be it resolved by the General Council of the Choctaw Nation assembled, That the report of Wallace Bond, District Collector of the First District, be and the same is hereby accepted as true and correct, And this resolution take effect from and after its passage.

Approved Oct. 2-, 1893.

W. N: JONES.
P. C. C N.

BILL NO. 22.

A resolution accepting the report of J. H. Miller, Inspector on the St. L. and S. F. R. R.

Your Committee to whom was referred the report of J. H. Miller, Inspector on the St. L. and S. F. Ry. have examined the same and find it to be true and correct, according to vouchers and reports as follews: Receipts for 1892, $19906.56· Receipts for 1893, $15,391.67 and ask the adoption of the following resolution:

Be it resolved by the General Council of the Choctaw Nation assembled, That the report of J. H. Miller, Inspector on the St. L. and S. F. Ry. be and the same is hereby accepted as true and correct, and this resolution take effect from and after its passage.

Approveed Oct. 24, 1893.

W. N. JONES,
P. C. C. N.

BILL NO. 23.

A resolution accepting the report of T. D. Ainsworth Superintendent of New Hope Seminary.

We your committee on schools to whom was referred the report of T. D. Ainsworth, Superintendent of New Hope Seminary, have examined the same and find it to be true and correct, with a balance on hand of twenty one and 42-100 ($21,42) dollars and ask the adoption of the following resolution to wit:

Be it resolved by the General Council of the Choctaw Nation assembled, That the report of T. D. Ainsworth, Superintendent of New Hope Seminary, be and the same is hereby accepted as true and correct, with a balance of twenty one and 42-100 ($21,42) dollars, and this resolution shall take effect from and after its passage.

Approved Oct. 23, 1893.

W. N. JONES,
P. C. C. N.

BILL NO. 24.

An Act relating to Simon McCoy District Collector of the Second District.

We your committee to whom was referred the report of Simon McCoy, District Collector of the Second District, have carefully examined the same and find that he is defaulter to the Nation for the sum of four hundred and sixty-six and 61-100 ($466.61) dollars and therefore would ask the adoption of the following Act:

Be it enacted by the General Council of the Choctaw Nation assembled, That the District Attorney of the Second District is hereby instracted to proceed at once by law against said Simon McCoy and his sureties on his bond for the collection of said sum and all proper costs and that the money so collected be turned into the National Treasury for National purposes. And this act take effect and be in force from and after its passage.

Approved Oct. 25, 1893.

W. N. JONES,
P. C. C. N.

BILL NO. 25.

An act appropriating $285.80, to pay P. J. Hudson, Superintendent of Tushka Homma Female Institute.

We your comittee on Schools, to whom was referred the report of P. J. Hudson Superintendent of Tushka Homma Female Institute, have examined the same and find that he has expended two hundred and eighty-five and 80-100 ($285.80) dollars over and above the amount appropriated: The above amount having been used as follows, to wit:—One piano, one team of mules, chairs, tables, screens, bath tubs, fourteen head of hogs, and work around the Academy, and ask the passage of the following act, to wit:

Be it enacted by the General Council of the Choctaw Nation assembled, That the sum of two hundred and eighty-five and 80-100 ($285.80) dollars be and the same is hereby appropriated out of any money in the National Treasury not otherwise appropriated to pay P. J. Hudson for money expended by him in the interest of the Tushka Homma Female Institute, and this act to take effect from and after its passage.

Approved Oct. 25, 1893.

W. N. JONES,
P. C. C. N.

BILL NO. 26.

A resolution accepting the report of J. W. Everidge, District Collector of 3rd Dist.

We your committee to whom was referred the report of J. W. Everidge, District Collector of the third District, have examined the same and find it to be true and correct and ask the adoption of the following resolution.

Be it resolved by the General Council of the Choctaw Nation assembled, That the report of J. W. Everidge, District Collector of the third District, be and the same is, hereby accepted as true and correct, and this resolution take effect and be in force from and after its passage.

Approved Oct. 25, 1893.

W. N. JONES,
P. C. C. N.

BILL NO. 27.

A resolution accepting the report of Robt. S. Frazier, District Collector of the second District.

We your committee to whom was referred the report of R. S. Frazier, District Collector of the the second District, have carefully examined the same and find it to be true and correct and ask the adoption of the following resolution:

Be it resolved by the General Council of the Choctaw Nation assembled, That the report of R, S. Frazier District Collector of the second District, be and the same is hereby accepted as true and correct, and this resolution take effect and be in force from and after its passage.

Approved Oct. 25, 1893.

W. N. JONES,
P. C. C. N.

BILL NO. 28.

A resolution accepting the report of W. W. Wilson, National Auditor.

Your committee to whom was referred the report of W. W. Wilson, National Auditor, have carefully examined the same and find it to be true and correct, and ask the adoption of the following resolution:

Be it resolved by the General Council of the Choctaw Nation assembled, That the report of W. W. Wilson be, and the same is hereby accepted as true and correct, and this resolution shall take effect and be in force from and after its passage.

Approved Oct., 25, 1893.

W. N. JONES,
P. C. C. N.

BILL NO. 29.

Be it enacted by the General Council of the Choctaw Nation assembled, That the sum of $50.00 be, and same is hereby appropriated out of any moneys not otherwise appropriated for the relief of Thomas Homa a deputy Sheriff of Atoka County, who was shot while discharging his official duty as such deputy, during the year 1892 to enable him to pay his indebtedness for medical attention and any other bills, and the Auditor is hereby authorized to draw his warrant on the Treasurer for the same.

Approved Oct., 25, 1893.

W. N. JONES.
P. C. C. N.

BILL NO. 30.

A resolution accepting the report of H. J. Kayser, Inspector on the C. C. and Ry. Co.

We your committee to whom was referred the report of H. J. Kayser, Inspector on the C. C. and Ry. Co., have carefully examined the same and find it to be true and correct, and ask the adoption of the following resolution:

Be it resolved by the General Council of the Choctaw Nation assembled, That the report of H. J. Kayser, Inspector on the C. C. Ry. Co., be and the same is, hereby accepted as true and correct, and this resolution to take effect from and after its passage.

Approved Oct., 26, 1893.

W. N. JONES,
P. C. C. N.

BILL NO. 31.

A resolution accepting the report of R. C. Robe Ex-Superintendent of Wheelock Seminary.

We your committee on schools to whom was referred the report of R. C. Robe, Ex-Superintendent of Wheelock Seminary have examined the same and find it to be true and correct, and ask the adoption of the following resolution:

Be it resolved by the General Council of the Choctaw Nation assembled, That the report of R. C. Robe Ex-Superintendent of Wheelock Seminary be and the same is hereby accepted as true and correct, and this resolution take effect and be in force from and after its passage.

Approved Oct. 26, 1893.

W. N. JONES,
P. C. C. N.

BILL NO. 32.

A resolution accepting the report of Henry Nail, Superintendent of Tushkalusa Academy.

We your committee on schools to whom was referred the report of Henry Nail, Superintendent of Tushkalusa Academy, have examined the same and find it to be true and correct and ask the adoption of the following rerolution:

Be it resolved by the General Council of the Choctaw Nation assembled, That the report of Henry Nail, Superintendent of Tushkalusa Academy, be and the same is hereby accepted as true and correct, and this resolution shall take effect and be in force from and after its passage.

Approved Oct., 26. 1893.

W. N. Jones,
P. C. C. N.

BILL NO. 33.

A resolution accepting the report of S T. Dwight late Supt. of Public Schools.

We your committee on Schools to whom was referred the report of S. T. Dwight, Ex-Supt. of Public Schools, have emamined the same and find it to be true and correct, and ask the adoption of the following resolution:

Be it resolved by the General Council of the Choctaw Nation assembled, That the report of S. T. Dwight Ex-Superintendent of Public Schools, for the scholastic year 1891-92, be and the same is, hereby accepted as true and correct, and this resolution take effect and be in force from and after its passage.

Approved Oct. 26, 1893.

W. N. Jones,
P. C. C. N.

BILL NO. 34.

An Act creating the office of National Inspector of Coal Companies books.

Sec. 1. Be it enacted by the General Council of the Choctaw Nation assembled, That the office of National Inspector of coal companies books be and the same is hereby created.

Sec. 2. That the duties of National Inspector shall be to inspect the books of the different Coal Companies of the Choctaw Nation; to make quarterly reports of the same to the National Treasurer, and annual reports to the General Council at the regular session: Same report to contain amount of royalty on coal, timber and permits due the Choctaw Nation.

SEC. 3. That the office of National Inspector shall be for a term of two years, and he shall be appointed by the Principal Chief, by and with the advice and consent of the Senate.

SEC. 4. That the National Inspector shall be required to take the oath of office prescribed in the Constitution, and enter into bond with good and sufficient securities in the penal sum of five thousand ($5000.00) dollars, payable to the Choctaw Nation, conditioned that he will well and truly discharge his duties in accordance with law.

SEC. 5. That the salary of National Inspector shall be one thousand ($1000.00) dollars per annum, payable quarterly, upou a warrant issued by the National Auditor upon the National Treasurer for the same. And this act shall take effect and be in force from and after its passage.

Approved Oct. 26, 1893.

W. N. JONES,
P. C. C. N.

BILL NO. 35.

Be it enacted by the General Council of the Choctaw Nation assembled, That Greenwood Leflore and his two children Nola and Louis Leflore be adopted as citizens of this Nation, and are hereby declared to be entitled to all privileges and rights of such citizens and this act take effect from and after its passage.

Approved Oct. 26, 1893.

W. N. JONES,
P. C. C. N.

BILL NO. 36.

Oct. 25, 1893.

To the General Council.

We the committee appointed to examine the report of E. N. Wright, National Agent, would report that we find his report in reference to royalties to be true and correct, The sum total is $130,156.32.

We further find that he has instituted proceedings to recover the amount due from the Choctaw Coal and Railway Co., as per act approved Nov. 3, 1892, and has received certificates of the receivers of the Choctaw Trading Company for 75 per cent of the true sum which is $9,370.05, which percentage is $7,027.54. Of this sum there was paid $702.75 as attorneys fees and $500 to McLeod & Lester the original attorneys employed previous to the passage of the act authorizing the employment of an attorney, and which was allowed by the Special Master in Chancery as their fee. Of the remainder, $5,500 is in receiver certificates, plus $324.79 in cash, which has been deposited in bank; due report will be made when the certificates have been foreclosed. The 25 per cent will be made out of Fritz Sittal individually. We would therefore recommend the passage of the following resolution:

Be it resolved by the General Council of the Choctaw Nation assembled, That the report of E. N. Wright, National Agent, be accepted as true and correct and this resolution be in force from and after its passage.

Approved Oct. 26, 1893.

W. N. JONES, P. C. C N.

BILL NO. 37.

A resolution adopting the report of E. S. Bowman, District Collector of the 1st District. To the General Council.

Your committee on finance, after having examined the report of E. S. Bowman, District Collector of the 1st District, carefully and impartially find the same to be true and correct and we respectfully ask the adoption of the following resolution:

Be it resolved by the General Council of the Choctaw Nation assembled, That the report of E. S. Bowman, District Collector of the 1st District, Choctaw Nation, be and the same is hereby accepted as true and correct and this resolution shall .. ..ect and be in force from and after its passage.

Approved Oct. 26, 1893.

W. N. JONES, P. C. C. N.

BILL NO. 38.

A resolution appropriating thirteen hundred dollars for Jones Academy and Tushka Homma Female Institute.

We, your committee to whom was referred the petitions of S. T. Dwight, Superintendent of Jones Academy and P. J. Hudson, Superintendent of Tushka Homma Female Institute, have examined the same and ask the adoption of the following resolution:

SEC. 1. Be it resolved by the General Council of the Choctaw Nation assembled, That the sum of thirteen hundred ($1300) dollars; six hundred ($600) dollars for Jones Academy to pay for cistern, and seven hundred ($700) dollars with which to pay for a furnace for Tushka Homma Female Institute, be and the same is hereby appropriated out of any money not otherwise appropriated for said academies.

SEC. 2. Be it further resolved, That the National Auditor is hereby authorized to issue his warrants to the superintendents of said academies, upon the treasurer for the said warrants and this resolution shall take effect and be in force from and after its passage.

Approved Oct., 27, 1893.

W. N. JONES,
P. C. C. N.

BILL NO. 39.

A resolution authorizing the National Treasurer to pay W. J. B. Lloyd $650 out of $700 appropriated for Armstrong Academy.

Be it resolved by the General Council of the Choctaw Nation assembled, That six hundred and fifty ($650) dollars be and the same is hereby appropriated for Armstrong Academy to pay W. J. B. Lloyd, and the National Treasurer is hereby directed to reserve and pay the same to W. J. B. Lloyd, and this resolution shall take effect and be in force from and after its passage.

Approved Oct. 27, 1893.

W. N. JONES,
P. C. C. N.

BILL NO. 40.

A resolution accepting the report of G. W, Thompson, Captain Militia 2nd District.

We, your committee to whom was referred the report of G.

W. Thompson, Captain Militia Second District, have examined the same and find it to be true and with a balance on hand of twelve (12) guns and ask the adoption of the following resolution:

Be it resolved by the General Council of the Choctaw Nation assembled, That the report of G. W. Thompson, Captain Militia of the Second District, be and the same is hereby accepted as true and correct with a balance of twelve (12) guns, and this resolution take effect and be in force from and after its passage.

Approved Oct., 27, 1893.

W. N. JONES.
P C. C. N.

BILL NO. 41.

An act making appropriation for the fiscal year ending July 31st 1894.

SEC. 1. Be it enacted by the General Council of the Choctaw Nation assembled, That the following sums are hereby appropriated for the general expenses of the Choctaw Nation during the fiscal year ending July 31, 1894, to-wit:

Principal Chief,	$2,000 00
Treasury, Auditor and Secretary	1,800 00
National Agent,	800 00
National Attorney,	400 00
Private Secretary,	500 00
National Light-horsemen,	2,450 00
Supreme Judges,	1,200 00
Circuit Judges,	1,500 00
County Judges,	4,250 00
District Chiefs,	150 00
District Attorneys,	950 00
Election judges and clerks,	680 00
Grand and petit juries,	14,900 00
Witness fees attending circuit court,	6,000 00
Superintendent of schools and trustees	1,800 00
Contingent Fund Chief,	400 00
" " Superintendent schools,	650 00
" " District trustees,	750 00

" " Auditor,	400	00
" " Treasurer,	400	00
" " Secretary,	400	00
Publication fund,	350	00
Clerks supreme court,	100	00
Clerks county courts,	1,700	00
Clerks circuit courts,	900	00
Sheriffs,	5,100	00
Rangers,	850	00
Sheriffs and deputies attending circuit court,	1,850	00
Deputy Sheriffs,	6,800	00
Sheriff attending supreme court,	50	00
General Council Lighthorsemen and clerk citizenship committee,	9,200	00
Students in states,	12,500	00
1st District neighborhood schools,	10,000	00
2nd " " "	9,000	00
3rd " " "	11,000	00
Spencer Academy,	10,000	00
New Hope Seminary,	10,000	00
Armstrong Orphan Home,	7,000	00
Wheelock Seminary,	5,600	00
Jones Academy,	10,000	00
Tushka Homma Female Institute,	10,000	00
Tushka Lusa Institute,	3,000	00
Teachers employees, Jones Academy, New Hope Seminary and Tushka Homma Female Institute,	5,850	00
Salary Superintendent Jones Academy, New Hope Seminary and Tushka Homma Female Institute,	3,600	00
Superintendent and teachers Tushka Lusa Institute,	750	00
Officers pro tem,	100	00
Mileage [illegible] lges,	100	00
Supreme court stationery,	25	00
Commissioner Chickasaw Nation,	255	00

SEC. 2. Be it further enacted that this act take effect and be in force from and after its passage.

Approved Oct., 27, 1893.

W. N. JONES,
P. C. C. N.

BILL NO. 42.

A resolution respecting the report of J. R. Lawrence, Inspector of D. & W. V. R. R.

Your committee on finance would respectfully report that J. R. Lawrence, Inspector on the D. & W. V. R. R., has not sent any report in for approval and we recommend the following resolution:

Be it resolved by the General Council of the Choctaw Nation assembled, That J. R. Lawrence, inspector on the D. & W. V. R. R. is hereby requested to send in his report for the past years service to the next session of the General Council of the Choctaw Nation. This resolution shall take effect and be in force from and after its passage.

Approved Oct. 27, 1893.

W. N. JONES,
P. C. C. N.

BILL NO. 43.

An act governing District Collectors.

Be it enacted by the General Council of the Choctaw Nation assembled,

SEC. 1. That the District Collectors shall make at the end of each quarter, a report of all moneys due from license traders under their supervision to the National Auditor and National Treasurer, and upon such statement the Auditor shall issue a warrant to such collector for his services, provided in no event shall a collector receive any money from any person, but the same shall be paid direct to the Treasurer.

SEC. 2. The collectors shall take sworn statements, before the county clerk of the county where the traders or contractor resides as to amount of tax due by them and shall send same to the National treasurer with his report.

SEC. 3. The first report under the provisions of this act

shall be made on the first day of January 1894, and every three months thereafter. The county clerk at said first day and every three months thereafter, shall be at the court ground for the purpose of administering oaths or in the absence of the collector, the parties knowing themselves to be indebted to the Nation, may go before the county clerk at the time of court and make affidavit as to the amount due and deliver such statement to the collectors The county clerk shall receive a fee of twenty-five cents (25) to be paid out of the National Treasury.

SEC. 4. And all acts or parts of acts coming in conflict with the provisions of this act are hereby repealed, and this act shall take effect and be in force from and after its passage.

Approved Oct. 27, 1893.

W. N. JONES,
P. C. C. N.

BILL NO. 44.

A resolution accepting the report of J. B. Jeter, Superintendent of Public Schools,

We, your committee to whom was referred the report of J. B. Jeter, superintendent of Public Schools, have examined the same and find it to be true and correct, with a balance on hand of five hundred and fifty ($550) dollars and ask the adoption of the following resolution:

Be it resolved by the General Council of the Choctaw Nation assembled, That the report of J. B. Jeter, superintendent of public schools, be and the same is hereby accepted as true and correct, with a balance on hand of five hundred and fifty ($550) dollars, and this resolution shall take effect and be in force from and after its passage·

Approved Oct. 27, 1893.

W. N. JONES,
P. C. C. N.

BILL NO. 45.

An act to authorize the Principal Chief to have the laws of the Choctaw Nation compiled, translated, printed and bound.

Be it enacted by the General Council of the Choctaw Nation assembled, That the Principal Chief be and he is hereby authorized to enter into contract with one competent person to compile, translate, print and bind in good substantial leather binding, five hundred copies each, in the English and Choctaw languages. Be it further enacted, That the amount stipulated in the contract above provided for shall not exceed four thousand dollars, and whatever may be stipulated in the contract, any part of which is not to be paid until the work has been completed and accepted as hereafter provided.

Be it enacted, that when the work is completed the compiler shall report it to the Principal Chief for inspection, and the Principal Chief shall appoint a committee of three competent persons and they shall investigate the work and report their investigation and if the work is accepted the Principal Chief shall issue a certificate to the compiler for amount under contract and the National Auditor shall issue his warrant for it and the National Treasurer pay the same.

Be it further enacted, That the work above provided for must be completed in a reasonable length of time, not to exceed four months from the date of the contract. The National Secretary is hereby required to furnish the compiler with all laws in his office whatsoever, in bound books, pamphlets or manuscript, and take receipts for them, and this act shall take effect and be in force from and after its passage,

Approved Oct , 27, 1893.

W. N. JONES,
P. C. C. N.

BILL NO. 46.

An act for the relief of H. T. Jackman.

Be it enacted by the General Council of the Choctaw Nation assembled, That the sum of eight dollars and thirty cents be appropriated for H. T. Jackman out of any money in the National Treasury not otherwise appropriated, for stationery used in the capitol, and this act take effect and be in force from and after its passage.

Approved Oct. 27, 1893.

W. N. JONES,
P. C. C. N.

BILL NO. 47.

An act for the relief of Martin Sexton, Student at Orleans, Illinois.

Be it enacted by the General Council of the Choctaw Nation assembled, That the sum of one hundred and fifty ($150) dollars be and the same is hereby appropriated out of any money in the National Treasury not otherwise appropriated, for the relief of Martin Sexton, a student of the Deaf and Dumb Institution at Orleans, Illinois, and upon the presentation of a certificate by the proper person or persons, having in charge the said Martin Sexton, the National Auditor shall issue his warrant upon the National Treasurer for the same. This act to take effect from and after its passage.

Approved Oct. 27, 1893.

W. N. JONES,
P. C. C. N.

BILL NO. 48.

An act in relation to neighborhood schools.

Be it enacted by the General Council of the Choctaw Nation assembled,

SEC. 1. That any neighborhood that employs a teacher shall be entitled to a neighborhood school, provided, however, that such schools shall not be nearer to each other than three miles measured along the most traveled wagon road, and provided further, that this limitation as to distance shall not apply to acknowledged towns. The provisions of this section are subject to the powers conferred upon the Board of Education by Sec. 3, Par. 8 and 9, Chap. 1, of act passed and approved Oct. 31st, 1890.

SEC. 2. That neighborhood schools shall be taught at least six (6) hours daily, Saturdays and Sundays excepted, during the term, and shall have regular hours of opening and closing. They shall open for the term on the first Monday of September and close on the last day of May in each year, but the District Trustee shall have power to grant school vacations and holidays at stated times during the term.

SEC. 3. That the benefit of a free neighborhood school

shall extend only to such Choctaw children as attend the schools within the Choctaw Nation established.

SEC. 4. That teachers in neighborhood schools shall be entitled to two ($2) dollars per month for each scholar in attendance, when such scholar has attended more than fifteen days in the month. But where the attendance has been less than fifteen days then such teacher shall receive ten (10) cents per day for each day of attendance, provided however, that teachers of the first grade shall not receive over forty-five ($45) dollars in one month, those of the second grade not over thirty ($30) dollars, and those of the third grade not over twenty ($20) dollars.

SEC. 5. That a scholastic month shall be taken and held to be of twenty days length.

SEC. 6. That teachers holding first grade certificates shall be examined every three years, teachers of second grade every two years, and teachers of the third grade, annually.

SEC. 7. That all acts or parts of acts coming in conflict with the provisions of this act are hereby repealed, and this act take effect and be in force from and after its passage.

Became a law by its own limitation. Nov. 1, 1893.

This is to certify that the foregoing is a true and correct copy of the original acts of the General Council of the Choctaw Nation now on file in my office.

Witness my hand and the Great Seal of the Choctaw Nation this the 2nd day of January A. D., 1894.

[SEAL.]

J. B. JACKSON,
National Secretary, Choctaw Nation.

The Acts of special Session in February 1892.

BILL NO. 1.

An act to comply with the requirements of an act of Congress approved March 3, 1891, making an appropriation to compensate the Choctaws and Chickasaws for their interest in the lands lying south of the Canadian river, and occupied under executive order by the Cheyenne and Arapahoe Indians, as modified by joint resolution of congress approved January 18, 1893, and for other purposes.

Whereas, an act of congress was approved by the President of the United States on the third day of March, 1891, containing the following provisions:

And the sum of two million, nine hundred and ninety-one thousand four hundred and fity dollars be, and the same is hereby appropriated out of any money in the treasury not otherwsie appropriated, to pay the Choctaw and Chickasaw Nations of Indians for all the right, title, interest and claim, which said Nations of Indians may have in and to certain lands now occupied by the said Cheyenne and Arapahoe Indians under executive order, said lands lying south of the Canadian river and now occupied by the said Cheyenne and Arapahoe Indians, said lands having been ceded in trust by article three of the treaty between the United States and said Choctaw and Chickasaw Nations of Indians, which was concluded April twenty-eight, eighteen hundred and sixty-six, and proclaimed on the tenth day of August of the same year; and whereof there remains, after deducting allotments as provided by said agreement, a residue ascertained by survey to contain two million three hundred and ninety-three thousand one hundred and sixty acres; three-fourths of this appropriation to be paid to such person or persons as are or shall be duly authorized by the laws of the Choctaw Nation to receive the same, at such time and in such sums as directed and required by the legislative authority of said Choctaw Nation, and one-fourth of this appropriation to be paid to such person or persons as are or shall be duly authorized by the laws of said Chickasaw Nation to receive the same, at such time and in such sums as directed and required by the legislative authority of said Chickasaw Nation. This appropriation to be immediately available and to become operative upon the execution by the duly appointed delegates of said respective Nations specially authorized thereto by law, of releases and conveyances to the United States of all the right, title, interest and claim of said respective Nations of Indians in and to said lands (not including Greer county which is now in dispute), in manner and form satisfactory to the President of the United States, and said releases and conveyances, when fully executed and delivered, shall operate to extinguish all claim of every kind and character of said Choctaw and Chickasaw Nations of Indians in and to the tract of country to which said releases and conveyances shall apply.

And whereas. The President of the United States approved January 18, 1893, the following joint resolution of congress:

Resolved, by the Senate and House of Representatives of the United States of America in congress assembled, That the Secretary of the Treasury be, and he is hereby directed to retain and cover back into the treasury forty-eight thousand and eight hundred dollars of the appropriation made by congress to pay the Choctaw and Chickasaw tribes of Indians for their interest in the lands of the Cheyenne and Arapahoe reservation, dated March third, eighteen hundred and ninety-one, which amount has been ascertained by a recount of the allottees of said Cheyenne and Arapahoes, to be by that amount more than is due the said Choctaws and Chickasaws upon the purchase and settlement for their said interest. Provided however, that neither the passage of the original act of appropriation to pay the Choctaw and Chichasaw tribes of Indians for their interest in the lands of the Cheyenne and Alapahoe reservation, dated March third, eighteen hundred and ninety-one, nor of this resolution shall be held in any way to commit the government to payment of any further sum to the Choctaw and Chickasaw Indians for any alleged interest in the remainder of the lands situated in what is commonly known and called the "leased district."

And whereas, The Choctaw Nation is ready and willing to sign, execute and deliver the releases and conveyances in said act mentioned, to the United States of the lands therein described, in manner and form satisfactory to the President of the United States.

Now, therefore be it enacted by the General Council of the Choctaw Nation assembled, That the said act of congress and said joint resolution, herein above mentioned, are hereby accepted and approved and that Green McCurtain, National Treasurer of the Choctaw Nation, or his successor in office, is hereby authorized to receive in behalf of the Choctaw Nation the amount appropriated in said act and joint resolution of congress, for and on behalf of said Choctaw Nation, for the interest in said lands, and said National Treasurer is hereby authorized to receipt in full to the Secretary of the Treasury of the United States, in the name of the Choctaw Nation therefor, provided that nothing herein shall be construed to impair any claim that the Choctaw Nation may have in any other than in what is known as the "leased district."

SEC. 2. Be it further enacted that Thomas D. Ainsworth, David W. Hodges and Green McCurtain, National Treasurer of the Choctaw Nation, or his successor in office, are hereby appointed delegates of said Choctaw Nation, with full power and authority to execute in the name of and on behalf of the Choctaw Nation, in manner and form satisfactory to the President of the United States, and to sign, seal and acknowledge the releases and conveyances described and mentioned in said part of said act of congress, and to deliver the same, when so executed, signed and acknowledged to the President of the United States, as and for the releases and conveyances of the Choctaw Nation, under said act and said joint resolution of congress of all right, title, interest and claim of every kind whatsoever of this Nation in and to the lands described in said act of Congress.

SEC. 3. And be it further enacted, That in case of the death, resignation or other inability of any of the said delegates to act as herein provided, the Principal Chief of the Choctaw Nation shall appoint and commission the proper person or persons to act as such delegate or delegates, for and on behalf of the Choctaw Nation with full power to carry out as such delegate or delegates the provisions of this act.

Approved Feb. 17, 1893.

W. N. JONES,
P. C. C. N.

BILL NO. 2.

An act for the relief of Tushka Homma Academy.

Be it enacted by the General Council of the Choctaw Nation assembled, That the sum of fifteen hundred dollars be and the same is hereby appropriated out of any money in the treasury not otherwise appropriated for the relief of Tushka Homma Academy in building a store and laundry house, etc.

Be it further enacted that the Auditor of the Choctaw Nation is hereby authorized to issue his warrant on the Treasurer for the same. This act is to take effect and be in force from and after its passage.

Approved Feb. 18, 1893.

W. N. JONES,
P. C. C. N.

BILL NO. 3.

An act appropriating to defray expenses of this session of Council.

Be it enacted by the General Council of the Choctaw Nation assembled, That the sum of fifteen hundred dollars be and the same is hereby appropriated to pay off the members and officers of Council for their services during this extra session and the National Treasurer is hereby authorized to pay the same out of any money not otherwise appropriated. That this act is to take effect and be in force from and after its passage.

Approved Feb. 18, 1893.

W. N. JONES,
P. C. C. N.

BILL NO. 4.

An act appropriating $8000 to defray the expense of guarding and boarding the prisoners at 1st District Court Ground.

Be it enacted by the General Council of the Choctaw Nation assembled, That the sum of eight thousand dollars be and the same is hereby appropriated out of any money in the treasury not otherwise appropriated, to defray the expenses of boarding and guarding the prisoners at 1st District Court Grounds up to May 15, 1893.

Be it further enacted, That after said expenses shall have been paid the balance of said appropriation shall be turned back into the treasury of the Choctaw Nation, and this act shall take effect and be in force from and after its passage.

Approved Feb. 18, 1893.

W. N. JONES,
P. C. C. N.

BILL NO. 5.

Be it resolved by the General Council of the Choctaw Nation assembled, That this special term of the General Council adjourn at 3 o'clock p. m., Feb. 18, 1893. And this resolution take effect and be in force from and after its passage.

Approved Feb. 18, 1893.

W. N. JONES,
P. C. C. N.

BILL NO. 6

An act appropriating $750 for pay for the superintendent and teachers at Tushkalusa Academy.

Be it enacted by the General Council of the Choctaw Nation assembled, That the sum of seven hundred and fifty ($750) dollars be and the same is hereby appropriated out of the National treasury, not otherwise appropriated, for pay of superintendent and teachers of Tushkalusa Academy.

Be it further enacted, That the National Auditor is hereby requested to issue a National warrant on the National Treasurer, and the National Treasurer pay the same and this act shall take effect and be in force from and after its passage.

Approved Feb. 18, 1893.

W. N. JONES,
P. C. C. N.

This is to certify that the foregoing is a true and correct copy from the original acts of the Special Session of Council now on file in my office.

[SEAL.] Witness my hand and the great seal of the Choctaw Nation this the 2nd day of January, A. D., 1894.

J. B. JACKSON,
National Secretary, Choctaw Nation.

THE ACTS OF SPECIAL SESSION IN JUNE 29, 1893.

BILL NO. 1.

An act designating places for distributing Leased District money.

Be it enacted by the General Council of the Choctaw Nation assembled,

SEC. 1. That in distributing or paying out the Leased District money the National Treasurer is hereby authorized to make the payment at such place or places in each district or county as may be most convenient to the beneficiaries.

SEC. 2. That the National Treasurer be and is hereby authorized and directed to employ fifteen men as guards during the payments at a compensation of two dollars and fifty cents per day each.

SEC. 3. That all acts and parts of acts in conflict herewith are repealed and this act take effect from and after its passage.

Approved June 29, 1893.

W. N. JONES,
P. C. C. N.

BILL NO. 2.

An act amendatory of the per capita act of April 1991.

Be it enacted by the General Council of the Choctaw Nation assembled, That in the revision of the several county lists of Choctaw citizens by blood to whom the Leased District money is to be paid, the revisory board consisting of the Principal Chief, National Treasurer, National Auditor and National Secretary, shall have authority to strike from the lists names which shall appear to them as manifestly not entitled to be on the lists, and shall also have authority to place such names on the lists as are manifestly entitled to be on them, but which have not been put on by the county commissioners of registration, provided however, that such action shall have the full concurrence of said revisory board. The county commissioners who bring the county lists to the capital shall remain to give needed information to the revisory board until the pay rolls prepared by and under the direction of the said revisorp board shall have been completed. The members of said revisory board and one commissioner from each county and one of the commissioners appointed to register Choctaw citizens by blood residing in the Chickasaw Nation, shall be entitled to $2.50 per day for every days service while engaged in preparing the pay rolls of the Choctaw Nation, the same to be paid on the certificates of the Principal Chief out of the fund already provided for expenses.

Approved June 29, 1893.

W. N. Jones,
P. C. C. N.

BILL NO. 3.

Resolution.

1. Be it resolved by the General Council of the Choctaw Nation assembled, That having full faith in the fitness and qualification of E. G. Douglas for the position of United States Marshal for the Eastern District of Texas we therefore recommend him on account of his integrity and uprightness and his fitness as above stated, to the President of the United States for said

position, and we further recommend him for such office for the reason that we believe and know that he will be acceptable to our people.

Be it further resolved, That our Secretary be required to furnish Mr. Douglass with a copy of this resolution under seal in order that the same may be presented to President Cleveland.

Approved June 29, 1893.

W. N. JONES.
P. C. C. N.

BILL NO. 4.

An act amendatory of the per capita act of April 11, 1891.

Be it enacted by the General Council of the Choctaw Nation assembled, That the per capita act approved April 11, 1891, be so amended so as at the end of first section, directly after the word "act" the following words be inserted, "nevertheless no person or pensons shall be entitled to participate in the per capita payment in both Nations," and this act shall take effect and be in force from and after its passage.

Approved July 1. 1893.

W. N. JONES,
P. C. C. N.

BILL NO. 5.

An act making appropriation to defray expenses of the militia

Be it enacted by the General Council of the Choctaw Nation assembled,

SEC. 1. That the sum of fifteen thousand ($15000) dollars is hereby appropriated out of any money in the treasury not otherwise appropriated, to pay the per diem and expenses of the militia in the late trouble at Antlers during the months of March and April A. D., 1893, and South McAlister, I. T., Sept. 1, 1892, and balance if any shall be refunded back into treasury.

SEC. 2. That this act be in force from and after its passage.

Approved July 1, 1893.

W. N. JONES,
P. C. C. N.

BILL NO. 6.

A resolution receiving the report of Green McCurtain National Treasurer.

Your committee on finance to whom was referred the report of Green McCurtain, National Treasurer, find the same to be true and correct with a balance on hand of $99,705 00. We recommend the passage of the following resolution:

Be it resolved by the General Council of the Choctaw Nation assembled, That the report of Green McCurtain, National Treasurer of the Choctaw Nation for 1891 Oct. 1, 1992, Oct 1, the same is hereby declared to be true and correct. This resolution to take effect and be in force from and after its passage.

Approved July 1, 1893.

W. N. JONES,
P. C. C. N.

BILL NO. 7.

A resolution receiving the report of J. W. Everedge

Your committee to whom was referred the report of J. W. Everedge, Collector in the 3rd District, find the same true and correct from July 31, 1891 to July 31, 1893, and we recommend the passage of the following resolution:

Be it resolved by the General Council of the Choctaw Nation assembled, That the report of J. W. Everedge, District Collector of the 3rd District, is hereby declared true and correct. This resolution to take effect and be in force from and after its passage.

Approved July 1, 1893.

W. N. JONES,
P. C. C. N.

BILL NO. 8.

An act making appropriation for C. S. Vinson and others.

Be it enacted by the General Council of the Choctaw Nation assembled, That the sum of thirty-one hundred dollars is hereby appropriated out of any money in the National Treasury not otherwise appropriated to pay C. S. Vinson, Joel W. Everedge, Green McCurtain and E. N. Wright, delegates or commissioners to Washington City in regard to the Antlers trouble—five hundred dollars each, also the sum of five hundred dollars to Ownby attorney, for service tocommissioners, and six hundred dollars to pay the expenses of said commissioners, in all thirty-one hundred dollars.

SEC. 2. That this act take effect and be in force from and after its passage.

Approved July 1, 1893.

W. N. JONES,
P. C. C. N.

BILL NO. 9.

TUSHKA HOMMA, I. T., NOV. 4, 1892.

TO THE GENERAL COUNCIL:

We the committee to whom was referred the report of J. H. Miller, Inspector on Frisco railway, would report that we have examined the same and from data at hand, we are not able to come to any final conclusion, according to thereport of said J. H. Miller there is a discrepancy of $6,088.36, according to the treasurers report the discrepancy is $4,818.13. We would therefore recommend the passage of the following resolution:

Be it resolved by the General Council of the Choctaw Nation assembled, That the report of J. H. Miller be laid over until next General Council, at which time the said J. H. Miller is instructed to produce all his receipts and vouchers of every kind for the inspection of the finance committee, and this resolution take effect and be in force from and after its passage.

Approved July 1, 1893.

W. N. JONES,
P. C. C. N.

BILL NO. 10.

A resolution receiving the report of E. S. Bowman; Inspector.

Your committee on finance after examining the report of E. S. Bowman, Inspector on San Francisco railroad for 1892, find the same correct, the receipts amounting to $510.78, and recommend the passage of the following resolution:

Be it resolved by the General Council of the Choctaw Nation assembled, That the report of E. S. Bowman, Inspector on the San Francisco railroad, is hereby declared to be correct and true, and this resolution to take effect and be in force from and after its passage.

Approved July 1, 1893.

W. N. JONES,
P. C. C. N.

BILL NO. 11.

A resolutiou receiving the report of W. A. Durant, Inspeetor on M. K. & T. Railway.

Your committee to whom was referred the report of W. A. Durant, Inspector on M. K. & T. railroad report that the same is true and correct and we beg that the following resolution be passed:

Be it resolved by the General Council of the Choctaw Nation assembled, That the report of W. A. Durant, Inspector on the M. K. & T. railroad from Nov. 1891 to July 31, 1892, is hereby declared true and correct. This resolution to take effect and be in force from and after its passage.

Approved July 3, 1893.

W. N. JONES,
P. C. C. N.

BILL NO. 12.

An act for the relief of J. W. Ownby. Esq.

Be it enacted by the General Council of the Choctaw Nation assembled,

SEC. 1. That the sum of twenty-five hundred ($2500) dollars be and the same is hereby appropriated out of any money in the treasury not otherwise appropriated, to pay J. W. Ownby of Paris, Texas, for his services as attorney, representing the Choctaw authorities in Washington City, on account of the late insurrection at Antlers.

SEC. 2. That this act take effect and be in force from and after its passage.

Approved July 3, 1893.

W. N. JONES,
P. C. C. N.

BILL NO. 13.

An act making appropriation to pay G. W. Dukes and A. R. Durant for leoal services rendered.

Be it enacted by the General Council of the Choctow Nation assembled, That the sum of one thousand dollars be and is hereby appropriated out of any money in the National Treasury not otherwise appropriated to pay Judge G. W. Dukes and A. R. Durant for legal services rendered in assisting Simon Lewis, District Attorney in and for the 1st Judicial District in prosecuting murderers in District Court in and for the 1st Judicial District of the Choctaw Nation.

Be it further enacted that the National Auditor is hereby directed to issue his warrant and National Treasurer pay the same, and this act shall take effect and be in force from and after its passage.

Approved July 3, 1893.

W. N. JONES,
P. C. C. N.

BILL NO. 14.

An act appropriating money to defray the expenses of guards at Wilburton Jail in the 1st District.

Be it enacted by the General Council of the Choctaw Nation assembled, That the sum of five thousand ($5000) dollars is hereby appropriated out of any money in the National Treasury not otherwise appropriated, to defray the expenses of guards at Wilburton jail in the first district, and this act shall take effect and be in force from and after its passage.

Approved July 4, 1893.

W. N. JONES,
P. C. C. N.

BILL NO. 15.

An act disposing of the fire-arms purchased by the Choccaw Nation for the Antlers trouble.

SEC. 1. Be it enacted by the General Council of the Choctaw Nation assembled, That the captains of the militia are hereby instructed to collect all fire-arms purchased by the Choctaw Nation for the use of the militia and return them to the capitol at Tushka Homma for storage. In case however, should any member of the militia prefer to retain said fire-arms, then he shall pay to the captain its value in money to be turned into the National Treasury, credit against the militia account and report by the next General Council.

Be it further enacted that this act be in force from and after its passage.

Approved July 5, 1893.

W. N. JONES,
P. C. C. N.

BILL NO. 16.

An act making appropriation to pay the expenses of the session of the General Council convened in June 1893.

Be it enacted by the General Council of the Choctaw Nation assembled, That the sum of three thousand ($3000) dollars be and the same is hereby appropriated out of any money in the National Treasury not otherwise appropriated, to pay members of extra session of General Council, its officers and Lighthorsemen in attendance; if any balance to be returned to the Treasury.

Be it further enacted that the Auditor is directed to issue his warrant on the National Treasurer and the National Treasurer pay the same, and this act take effect and be in force from and after its passage.

Approved July 5, 1893.

W. N. JONES.
P. C. C. N.

This is to certify that the foregoing is a true and correct copy from the original acts of the extra session of the General Council now on file in my office.

[SEAL.] Witness my hand and the great seal of the Choctaw Nation, this the 2nd day of January, A. D., 1894.

J. B. JACKSON,
National Secretary, Choctaw Nation.

INDEX.

	Page
Appropriation—for special session	40
Appropriation—for Militia	35
Adjournment—Resolution of	32
Ainsworth, T. D.—Report of	13
Adjournment—Resolution of	12
Appropriation—for schools	20
Appropriation—for fiscal year	21
Appropriation—for special session	31
Boarding Schools—in relation to	11
Bond, Wallace—Report of	21
Bowman, E. S.—Report of	19
Bowman, E. S.—Report of	37
Coal weigher—Abolishing office of	11
Chickasaw Commission—Relating to	8
Citizenship—Albert Leflore, et al	1
Caldwell, W. A.—Report of	3
Court Ground—Change of	5
Durant, W. A.—Report of	38
Dukes & Durant—Relief of	39
Dwight, S. T.—Report of	2
Delegate to Congress—Creating office of	6
Dwight, S. T.—Report of	17
District Collectors—Governing	23
Douglas, E. G—Recommending	34
Ellis, C. N.—Report of	7
Everedge, J. W.—Report of	14
Everedge, J. W.—Report of	36
Floating of Timber—Preventing of	7
Frazier. Robt S.—Report of	15
Fire-arms—Sale of	39
Guards Wilberton—Relief of	32

Guards Wilburton—Relief of - - - - - - 39
Henry, Amos—Report of - - - - - 3
Hudson, P. J.—Relief of - - - - - - - 14
Homma, Thos.—Relief of - - - - - - 15
Inspector of Coal—Creating office of - - - 17
Jeter, J. B.—Report of - - - - - - - 24
Jackman, H. T.—Relief of - - - - - - - 25
Kayser, H. J.—Report of - - - - 16
Leased District Money—Ralating to - - - - - 33
Leased District—Relating to - - - - - - 28
Laws—Compilation of - - - - - - - 24
Law Books—Sale of - - - - - - - 5
Leflore, Greenwood—Citizenship of - - - - 18
Lloyd, W. J. B.—Relief of - - - - - - 20
Lawrence, J. R.—Report of - - - - - - - 23
McCurtain, Green—Report of - - - - - 9
Miller, J. H.—Report of - - - - - - - 37
Miller, J. H.—Report of - - - - - - 12
McCoy, Simon—Report of - - - - - 13
McCurtain, Green—Report of - - - - 36
Nail, Henry—Report of - - - - - 17
Neighborhood Schools—Relating to - - - 27
Ownby, J. W.—Settlement with - - - - - - 1
Ownby, J. W.—Relief of - - - - - 38
Percapita Act—Amending - - - - - - - 35
Riddle, D. A.—Report of - - - - - - 4
Robe, R. C.—Report of - - - - - 16
Standley, J. S.—Relief of - - - - - 4
Sexton, Martin—Relief of - - - - - - 26
Tushkahomma Academy—Relief of - - - - 31
Toll Bridge—Perry Creek privileges - - - - 2
Thompson, G. W.—Relief of - - - - - - - 9
Thompson, G. W.—Report of - - - - - 20
Teachers Tushkahomma School—Relief of - - - 32
Vinson, C. S.—Relief of - - - - - - 36
Wilson, Ed—Report of - - - - - 4
Wilson, W. W.—Report of - - - - - 15
Wright, E. N.—Report of - - - - - 18

DATE DUE

GAYLORD PRINTED IN U.S.A.

WITHDRAWN
FROM
NEW MEXICO STATE UNIVERSITY
LIBRARY